WHISPERS

&

SOUNDS

RON BARTALINI

Sundie Enterprises
Since 1972

Sundie Enterprises
P.O. Box 1274
Provo, Utah 84603-1274

ISBN 978-0-9859811-4-3
Library of Congress Card Catalogue Number:
2015919609
Bartalini, Ron

Description: A quiet look at the sudden
stillness of nature. Memories of the sometimes
surreal, college life of the 60's told with words that
make sounds and may allow the reader to
experience a lovely taste of déjà vu. A series of
poems started in California, continued on the
American River College campus, Brigham Young
University, Rhode Island, Nova Scotia and New
Brunswick, Canada. Written from 1964-1968.

1. Whispers—Poetry 2. Sounds—Poetry
3. Onomatopoeia—Poetry 4. Nature--Poetry
1. Bartalini, Ron

WHISPERS

The Walk

The opening of midnight
an oak tree is now wiser
than the owl
that only sits.

The Jack Rabbits are
even aware of me
as I watch in silence.

The opening of midnight
I am no longer profound.

The ending of sunlight,
the palette of the sky
changes hues
before
my amazed
eyes.

The opening of midnight
I am no longer profound.

The squirrels that have
labored all the day long-
to have been but half
destroyed by
calf boys
with twenty-two rifles are
either in bed
or dying.

My imagination that
watches the dove
fly by, then softly
light against the sky
is now alive-

Exciting
is
a word that helps,
awesome, perhaps
incomprehensible
is this time of day.

The opening of midnight
I am no longer profound.

I walk upon my first
used path back to my
shelter.
There are
other
marks that comfort
mine.

Others have made their way past
my experience-
they perhaps noticed more than I.

My gun is cold upon
my shoulder.
Its muzzle
was once
warm today
reaping the fruits
which God
provides.

My ears are cold too-
they are now chilled
by the same
kind of wind
that woke me.

The opening of midnight
I am no longer profound.

If I were wise and old
perhaps I would
know what I have
seen today.
Were I
a scholar
I might understand
how the sun was made
and why it warms
us
at
daytime.

I might know of the soil
I have trodden
and how it works.

I might know
many things
if I were
an
old man.

The closing of midnight
I am becoming profound.

Why Is
the Whole World
Dead?

Why is the whole world dead?
Why do people just sit and stare?
Why does no one seem to care?
Why is the whole world dead?

Stillness

When all is still
there is peace at last
and one can here the insects pass
and feel the wind
and taste the breeze
and listen to the rustling leaves.

But even stillness can't endure
for man has made
his presence sure
and though for interaction
an excellent cure
man is here, but peace, not for sure.

And so what is man to do
most assuredly he cannot sue

and so endure he must
till his dying day
when all of worry
is cast away...on earth.

But the leaves yes, the leaves will
always blow
And those who watch will
always know.

That peace and stillness
are here each day
and though man must die
what of stillness?

The Peach Tree

In front of me, a near dead sky
black, dismal and blue grey
save those few bright eyes
of Christ like light
that speeds your heartbeat
on its way.

Below, telephone wires
that dangle
helplessly
and lead to where anyone's guess
would have them lead.

Just as fast the black gives way
and in that moment a gull
soars skillfully
then falls away.

The wind that comes
this time each year
is here today.
Leaves that months ago were bright
are loosing their struggle to survive.

Doors swing open,
sway,
then smash shut
and the soft, pink roses
all close up-
to only crumple
back to dust.

To my right
the wind blows slowly
then fast.

With bursting, surging, wailing blasts
of flapping, slapping,
surging strength
that ends with all green things
near faint.

Blue and purple shades of gray
have brought with them
this day's
end.

Yet in front, the peach tree stands
with leaves but enough
to fill
each hand.

That same peach tree
has still the night
and will all nights
till cold, black eves
and dreary skies
bring fresh new fruit
in months like
July.

As Crowds They Wet

On my windshield, drops of rain
that will plummet once again
and
again.
Terribly common and impersonal
as crowds they wet
yet not so ugly as
summer sweat.

Hello, you diamond drop
fresh smelling
not like the clock.

"Swish, swash," go wiper blades
that lash
your backs like slaves.

Poor, pretty sparkling things
your beauty dies
for
lesser kings.

Stop.
I'll end that biting blade
should rather strain my sight
instead.

But wait,
sweet, helpless drips that came.
You feel no hurt, no life,
no pain.
just rain, that's all you are.

Rain that falls from
near high as stars.
You give life
not feel it.

No fate, no chance
for
rain.
You will only fall again.

I can't control you
but merely adore you
from your heaven
till
your
end.

And so
dear guided bits of sea
walking endless paths like we.
Why leave?

Surely your place
is closer to Him.
And so
why leave?

Oh, that's right
now
I see.

Pure and Simple Truth

In a room of many streets I dwell,
seeking avenues and minds.
The shelves inside of a closed box
of sun cloud tablets number
from Sophocles and further,
to the curious crew
of half mossed over youth
and
wooden silence.

The kind of page thumbing
and erasing that doesn't wake you.

The sort of paper crumbling
and tip toeing
that comforts some
irreplaceable necessity
for order and pencils handed in on
time
and kept sharp
and underlined until the ink runs dry.

Here I muse in the latency of living.
Seeing on occasion another
inquisitive eye
but mostly, gliding empty passers by
continuing to daily die.

And I, the poet,
the observer of coughs
and red socks that are
completely out of place
with any fashionable match,
admit that as I write,
I too, must burst
but life at best is lived.

Life is best walked through
fully awakened, deeply knowing
all things
but most perfectly perhaps,
the
You.

It is not passion
that carries me on
nor a computed equasion
that brings a new sky
filled with hues of love,
and a reflection
of man's
eternal existence.
This is not a state of breathing
by have nots and can nots
or did nots
but merely
the velvet-laden hills of pure
and
simple truth.

October Wind

The glad winged flapping pigeons
hushing on wind
that touches my face softly
and an orchestra
of yellowed autumn leaves
serenade me
with
their
silent music.

Ah, the soft, the gentle
October wind.

The stately green
and soldiered forest.

Amazed ah, I stand amazed!
October moment
with the
grand canyoned echoes
of children
playing and running
back
to
their
books.

Again
the silence.
Eternal and profound
grassing on the leaflets
standing by me.

Adam's Tune

How long ago
did the four winds blow?
How long ago
was
the first winter's day
that Father Adam felt
as he
mused away?

And God said,
"Let there be light
And there was light."

And God said,
"Let there be lights
in the firmament of the heaven
to divide the day from the night
and let them be
for signs and for seasons
and for days
and
for
years."

How long
have they been here
the seasons
and times?

God's book says from eternity
without beginning or end.

And yet even the poet
sees the change of the sands
and the river that changes
and the oncoming clouds
that renew
the land
and age-
the changing of you
and man.

And so we know
this masterful orb
will change,
will change
will change again.

Sannie

Sannie is a mountain
all seasons beholding.
Music is her language
she speaks seven kinds
softly and easy
as autumn leaves
fall by me.

When I Came Back Home

My many nighted merrily walkings
cantalouped by the blackbird sky
after the drunkards have filled
my eyes and I've gone home.

Recalls of my youthful youth
and the things I saw
and knew were truth.

Now worlds apart
I still wince to see
the midnight
start to close in on the souls
of
men.

And the gasps
and the whispers
and the enticing
and the lies
of Beelzebub
draw them all down quietly
to
hell.

Like Candles Shine

Somewhere beyond the stars
beyond the clustered
memory ships
the voice of the Lord
comes through
comes through, I say.
I hear it
the voice of my God
never failing.

A Letter to A Friend

Telephoto wings of people
sighing
saying Mary's gone away.
Singing nuns
those certainly purple people
silently passing the morning away
and I'm gone with the sadness
of
your
song.

Often the shadows fall down
all over my face
and remind me
to say,
"I loved her one time
I told her my mind.
She loved me her way."

More Aware

I grow tired
of boots that walk
the same
chains that are fastened
behind.

I marvel at a lunch bag
eating alone
in a corner-
watching something
other than
the apple
inside.

I like a tie
that doesn't fit
a coat or the neck
it squeezes.

I even like *Tump Heads*
who climb over chains
and say they hate poetry.

I like anything that speaks
with all of its senses-
anything that
breathes for twenty-four
hours and lets
the flowers provide
the air.

Two Pods on A Pea

Once a salt and pepper
shaker waited to be
tipped.

They knew what they
had to offer
the air
and whatever else
used them
but they were
full
and the air around them
was being used up
and
re-used.

Flowers didn't use much
but what a shame
that whatever
some breathers
want
some
exhalers get.

Moods of My Mind

Moods of my mind
wheat fields-
poster paints and you
were mine
my crime-
the lights of time
grew dark.

A day-
snow blown
and dark.
A mountain
an icy stream
the park
I've been through
before
and you
weren't there.

My canvass looks at
where you were
and finds another.
Its face remembers
you and my guitar
recalls now and then.
Your ways have not changed
but mine.

You've given much
my mind thinks
of others.
The things I do
help me to
remember-
someone
like
you.

Christmas

Autumn's pretty dress has fallen.
All the spooks
and goblins are solemn.
Turkey feasts have been forgotten.
Christmas has its special problem.

Day's are shorter, darker, colder
but fireplaces have hot coals
and there are electric blankets
and
under clothes.

Children's lists are wider, longer
but there is credit close at hand
and green stamps
and installment plans.

Parties, bourbon, scotch and gin
secretaries ponder sin
weekend visits to the snow
anticipated
stockings full.

Spending, giving, owing, receiving
delighting, exchanging,
pretending amazed.
Christmas is all of this and more.

Pity the poor
they can't buy Christmas.
Do not envy the rich who can.

But admire men
who really
understand
for the meaning of Christmas
is far out of hand.

Sailing

Till heaven's felt
the lifelong gale
I sail my ship a dreamin'
through mystic lands
of spices
all frankincense
and myrrh.

To All My Friends

I once saw the rainbow
of my imagination
and then it disappeared.

I once wrote a million songs
and now I am re-writing
them all.

For I found out today
that time began somewhere
besides-
in me
and
around
me.

I am asleep and dreaming
with my eyes wide open.

My friends
I have known you all
at
another sphere.

Within a season
we'll meet again.

We have the same likes
that must mean something.
What
is It
about living
that seems eternal anyway?

Emotional Merry Go Round

Please tell me why
the moon shines so bright
and
all
the world
is sleeping?

Is there any time
for
turning me on?

My bird is far away.
I'm standing here alone
watching silent children
building snowmen two feet high.
Listening to the sounds
snowflakes make
as they glide past my eyes.

Hey!
I was aware of this before.

Give me a word to say it with-
love.
Love is the only word that explains
everything.

Watching little children
fade away.
It's dark outside
the day is changing.

Love's Flowers

Way out in a field of flowers
I count every petal
and hold on to
my
kite string.

Just like a mountain
spring time.

I feel the soft wind
breezing by me
something free as seagulls
graceful
I'm walking slowly
holding the flowers we picked.

Watching your hair blowin' easy
thinking of sunsets
and rainbows
walking by a
silent brook.

We stopped
and saw the reflection
of love's
flowers.

Looking Through
That Apartment Window

Sometimes when you're sad
every day the wind blows
and ice is still
on the tops of lakes
frozen.

The only warmth to be found
is
the music
that soothes you
and when you're outside
alone and cold
you can't begin
to take that warm feeling
home.

Standing on a mountain
full of snow
with one
winter flower.

Ice skates against frozen mirrors
then
one snowflake.

The unseen observer
may be unseen
but he must speak.

Love is like a meadow
that stretches
to
the sea.
You look so wonderful to me
come closer my love.

My love is like a seashell
glistening in her maiden beauty.

A teaspoon of praise
at the right instant
is the
final ingredient
to
the
greatest recipe
for
success.

The Beauty
of the Professor

Ah, the beauty of the professor.
The poetry
of bewildered eyes.
Staring eyes
through book worn glasses.
Glasses that have read a wealth of
fine print
and never tired of learning.

The beauty of
his
spoken voice.

.

A shallow voice
filled by time yet fading.
I listen and begin to swell
from
the music
within
me.

I look and I see and I run
faster than ever before
that I might catch
such knowledge
and bring songs to others
who
wait with their ears.

Ode to A Sandy Girl

You-
girl I do not know
but of your face
the idea of you
has been on my mind
for as long as my eyes
have seen you
and more.

The first whisper of your
voice-
the words you uttered
your eyes were moist
and you knew not.

And I have been
trying to understand
your
explanation.

Your need to tell me
what you did
not knowing
who
I was at the time.

I have been trying
to understand everything
you did that day
but if I never do
I will always love
the air around
your kind.

Instructions for Living

Wash your mind out
with soap my friend
and pray that you will
always brush your teeth
each day-
think of painting
In the morning-
music at night
and
you
for
noon.

Whisper, But Not So Fast

The upcoming sky
benevolent
virtuous.
Float you a song
from the midst
of
my ocean.

Far away
look to the west wind.

The symmetry
of a billion
expanding stars.

Never a daydream
so sudden-
goodbye.

& SOUNDS

Once Upon Gazing

The Pop Art show was noisy
goofy and scare crows written
on
tabletops smelt hungry.
Heaps of sausage steaks
squashed flatter than
hamburger pancakes
were making time
somewhere or at every
table.

The crooked nosed girl
had pretty strands of hair.
Her tablet writing
broke her nails.

"P. J. and M. I.,"
spoke the tabletop
to
my face.

"Bark, ruff," went Pluto.
so many intelligent witticisms
that
poets
feel incompetent.

What a conversation piece
this room!
The prophet and his bride
in sandals have gone.
My milk shake
appears edible.
Pity-
the polka dot
bopper has a hurt
patella.

Look a likes were they all
and even
my speaking cloth top
with
hearts.

"So many roving eyes too,"
the light bulb
has spoken.

"Peggy Jolly is a real
beauty."

"Here lies the body
of an auto,"
said another square.
"Me too," went the
arrow.

The gone blonde
disappeared through
the wall.
"Blast!" Went the walls
in
regret.

The inky, pink
in vogue shopper followed
in
second hand clothes.

72 footballs slid
along
to
a sidewalk.
"Two booths next
to another, please."
"But they're not,
Mary Rawson."

"Red light
70 Ekins Court,"
went the tabletop again.

A saxophone disagreed
and screamed,
My World Is Empty
Without
You Babe.

"Stop!"
The patella has healed.
A violin voice of 17
turned the room into
a soft
summer night.

A night of
city girls
without
glasses.
But only
checkerboard smiles.

21 years ago
the tabletop
would not have spoken
such blue blooded
words.

But now inclined to
limousines
and picnic scenes
life has changed its mind.

It was a very good year
17.
Aw, the violins
have never stopped
they never lived
but will.
Some day,
one moment.

To imagine this
will be.
Here lies the body
of
a flea.

Such
sweet adventure.
Life is such rainbows.
The secret of it all
is the
miracle
of what
tabletops can do.
Ann and Dale.
Mandy
and me.
Boys-
bully wooly
apple aplanelappy.

Flyer

Sound of
silence.
'Twas too warm
for
Greeks.
The room of tennis shoed
girls and soda
was noisy
with trumpets
that stopped
then started again.

The pizza walker
must have walked
a million miles
on roads
made for athletes
and not shampoo fans.

Suddenly Astrid Gilberto
broke the silence
for connoisseurs
but just until an anxious
crier
sang, *Thrill Me*
to
the
third power.

Be
sensible
daydream love-
but not
in
the dark.
Kiss me through
infinity.
People need people-
not sounds of
promise.

Turn on Your Light

If your star falls out
of the sky-
scream at it
and make it come back.

If it seems gone
forever,
turn on your light.

A Walk in the Morning Without Walking

All my benighted
memory walks.
Platitudes against
séance and skilled
un toddlers
baby carriaging it along at daytime
in sea time
in afternoon song.
Sun stroken by timekeepers
in opportasty apparel.
Squeezing the last sound of the
morning quick
crow.

The rooster of egg fame
that bellows a blow
a familiar and latency wakening
"cock a do," cock a do-
cock a doodle, doodle do."

A nipsy nape flyer
that warbles in tune.

All my frettings
all of
them too.
All the begats and begettings of you
and June weds who wed up too
family treed soon.

All of my hastenings-
hastening
croons.
Sing you
a star edged
a rarified
tune.

A singsong,
a bird song
a sartorial
groove.

Catch you a morning
a gull
on
the wing.

A season, a wave capped
with turquoise of rain
and mists of profusion
all spangled with spoons.

The polliwogging,
Christmas logging
fir treed dragoons.
Sing you an ocean
a syrup train of plumes.
Sound out the off mate,
the Pearliwink's bloomed.

Memories of Ice Skating in Nova Scotia

My stars of the morning
all nestled
in lacy
apparel.

Nestle up a little closer
and feel like a sparrow.
'Twas certainly skating
I was at the time.
I wasn't misgiving her fortune
to
mine.

A snow flaked emotion
fell into my face.
An avalanche of pillow's feathers
least they looked
that way
but softer and cold
easy cold
on
my cheeks.
I washed up much faster
when I ate Mildred's cheese.

Then back to Mrs. Potter
and rolling ice skates
it was fun by the fires
inside of
tires.

At night-when the dogs
got our legs
we used them to rest on.
Sometimes we skated right into
the dawn.
Cross country like and athlete
in
a ripe
marathon.

It was eternal
intricate fun.
Seemed to be fastest
when someone would willow like
the willow tree
and fall down and get up
right next
to me.

And we'd fall down again
a slippery game-
ice inner tube skating
a national
name.

Came then a young bird
and collided with ease
and broke up some eye glasses
which landed in
Mildred's
cheese.
Ah, time for the soup bowl
and back to the fire,
to fill up a new lazy
nocturnal
warm dryer.

Behold the Ants with Ties

The flow of life around me
the tendons of humanity
confound the sanctity of priests.

Helpless almost, to trespass
the hoax of flooding,
inflating,
frustration.

Parts of no anatomy that
exist for real, for touch
but live only as an
organic lump of sugar in
a turtle's
helmet shell.

"Help," Scream the ants with ties
to themselves and inside
but hungry for tea leaves-
fortune.

Tides of burning
sunspots
more vast than a million
harlots cannot be ignored.

The Inlander

Hark, the inlander-
the sullen shadowed streetwalker
comes from midnight to eternity
and walks on every flattened
way the earth provides.
Alone, blissful, remembering
shaving nights and showers
careless hours of
awakening to the symphony
of birds and golden liars.
Forgotten-
midnight
and
the black
cold air.

Before Loneliness

Once happy before loneliness
was known
babies cried
and
you too.

A Big Pink House

A big pink house made noise
in
my ear.
Peopled passers ponged on
marshmallow stairs
with fragile toes-
flowing like watermelons
down
a
dry thorax.

A soft white blonde
is the
past end
of goes

and there are sandwiches
walking in clothes
on their toes
on the
candy cane roads.

Little blue skirts
made of pineapples
and zinc
slid on their sleds
and the violins appear
and disappear
in
the
big
pink house.

If I didn't know better
I'd call you a louse
you criticizer of artisans
Plato and Faust.
You donate your walls
and your rooms for the joust
and all you are
is
a big
pink house.

Gloria Gills

An ultra sonic boom
was discerned
from Gloria Gills
the pusher.

It's saddening to see
that her lemons ran out.

What an achievement!
Gloria's gills
are turned
inside out!

Red Jacket Lad

Oh, red jacket lad
in slovenly dress
why worry for finances, rainbows
and cash.

You're happy as a doorknob
that's daily turned.

Why worry for changing-
when for your free life
the other part yearns.

Fairy Tale Maiden

Eat away young fairy tale maiden.
Drink down each drop
from
the cup
of
experience.

Life but begins
with each new sun
and remember these words:
"No two children
see the same things.
No two artists have the same eyes."

The Young Man's Clock

Through city streets
once walked a young man
carrying his clock without recording.

Timeless, carefree,
pausing just for yawning.

The young man woke
with the cock's crow
hungry
restless
for
new things
to
feel.

Eager for new fantasies
to begin
but afraid, not then
that they would end.

Day upon day
and year upon year's end
clocked
the
timeless ticker.

Measuring out
boy's lives
like so many lumps
to the teaspoon
of
sugar.

Lilly Pad Linda

Skinny Lilly Pad Linda
likes seven lumps
of sugar in her
lunch pail
dinners.

She eats them all down
with one
gapping growl.

Zoom

Beneath sudden shadow
and tides of half forgotten
lip felt moments I rest
to pause on the singularity
of life's
physical self.

Here
in the midst of music laden rooms
the past zooms free
in front of me
and all eternity
is seen just passing
changing
empty.

Hark

The resounding
trumpet.
The chunky goose girls
be blowing the cows
home from mountaintops again.

Infinitesimal fatness
expressive
nasal
breaths
of
blah,
blah,
blah.

Hurry the tide rises.
Next, the oncoming
moon time
singing mooing songs
to
the night.

Cleaning Woman

Clop
the schoolboy goes
crowding in dozened droves
through half bright
Picasso covered caverns.

The cleaning woman
hanging to the rail
watches each reflection.
It beats washing windows.

Broom sweepers are cleaning
the big old house
even carpets get swept.

All for bumbling
brief cases that clop rain
muddied blobs
on
the tile.

Take a rest cleaning woman.
Use the softest new sofa
but clean it when you leave.

Don't speak to the performers.
Better yet
go home early.

Schoolboys

This wooden society
has its core
explained in words
plastic, sudden
frozen In every schoolboy's seat.

And the wooden chairs
are sanded down fine
shellacked to a worn away
gloss from rebelling bottoms.

"Help," the schoolboys scream
with words half censored
and cluttered
upon
columns.

Everyone reads,
then coughs with a laugh inside.
Don't breathe too loud
the crowds will hear.

Don't let them touch you
they'll get splinters.

Don't touch them
you might change.

The Big Jet Flew Away

Whiskered and weary I sit
with a query
and wonder while someone
ca choos.

I can hear thunder
all blowing asunder
I wonder who's riding caboose?

"Help!" sang the monsters
and I watched them captured
and then the big jet flew away.
Up like a partridge
a warbling yardage
of
violet
isotope bouquets.

Lately As My Mind Wanders

When the time is right
I put my hands over my head
stretched upwards
and I just fly.

I'm a boy in a bubble
then, I'm a boy in flight.

What a pretty lively
watching the world
pass us by from the tiptop
of my bubble in the sky.

Oh, but it's so much nicer
when someone else
is in your bubble with you
and you two can see through
the
same eyes.

What a lovely way
to glide through the mysteries
and realities of crimson life
it tis a merry gold vacation
I perceive it tis.

Almost just like Alice in Wonderland
jumping down that rabbit hole
to a new world,
well, my world's in the sky.

Oh, how I love gliders and sail boats
and kites and sitting up
against a tree by a mountain stream
and thinking and seeing and feeling
and living
life.

Ah, yeah, that's the way
the dandelions fly
and so do I.
People will say I'm daffy
but I feel for their hearts

and their ears
and their senses
and I know why,
cause once I didn't care for them
but now I serve my fellows.

And with that I'm high...
high from giving of myself
and do you know why
good fair presently confused
good guy
or princess
or maiden
of
the sky?

Oh, how I love the sky.
I once painted it when I first arrived
into this cerulean
and mortal
life.

That's when I still remembered
the before of my life...
My star
studded memory
impregnates my mind with recalls
of my ever clearer before life
and I can see much more clearly
forward and into my new life-
yet I oft times wonder in awe
is it all the re-doings,
the re-enacting
of the before
my physical self arrived?

Are
you still there
fond reader
or have you yet arrived-
are we yet together-
in thought
and mind?

I certainly do hope and approve
if you're right bout the fleeting
of emotions
that wanders into the night.

You know alone time is think time
and sometimes
tis
all right.

Yet together time
when you think time
is the highest form
of life
and the virtue that exists
from a listener
is Truth
most eternal
most forcefully sublime.

You see my fond feather
my sweet budding petal of life
so right and firm and ripe
with the making of a new life
inside
only when there are two
in the bubble
can you
really see life.

Do ya see, do ya sense,
do ya feel this is right?

And deep within the physical identity
of the to be man
and his wife
is
a beautiful, spiritual
you
and it is exactly the same
as I look through your eyes...
I can even begin to remember
your mind and your temperament
and your character
and your lines of identity
they were just the same
as that which is before my eyes.

Are you now yet with me?
Dear reader
dear searcher or dearest daughter
of a
celestial life?

Ah, but tis most wonderful
and deliciously right
that only when the bubble bursts
can Father begin
a new life
cause if there were no bubbles
and people to fill them
there'd be no reason for life.

Now I'm on a mountain
in a garden of flowers
flyin' kites and writing
the songs of my heart
to this life
and the breeze becomes
softer on my face
and on my kite
then faster
and I fly away
through the sky
and race deep into my mind
and that's when I begin
to discover new traces
of me and the before
this physical, most more
emotional life.

And now are you with me
dear searcher?

There's not much more
I can tell at this time.
Ah, yet the whisperings
of the spirit to my spirit
through time
all day will make me wonder
how short time ago
I too raced myself through time
and perhaps and most assuredly
with my arms over my head
stretched out wide.
Tis not the murmurings of a
daft or a silly fellow
with a warped mind
but yet the truth
eternal
and sublime.

Uncle Mary

Shucks
Uncle Mary
you didn't have to
sing short wave radio.
Tenor
would have been
just fine.

Forecast

Bring on the eggs
my days of the morning
sun fortuned misused
foreordained rain
with chance of clearing
otherwise
cloudy.

Heflin Arbuckle

Oh, Heflin Arbuckle
the little weed doth
gone a mowin'.

Ten Cherubs ever mysterious
watching nearby inquired,
"Ello Sir Heflin Arbuckle.
owls the legs feel
on
your
marshmallow stairs?

"Legs ain't what
they used to be,"
says Heflin.

Oh, Heflin Arbuckle's what he was
all right.
A toot tea toot
tea too.

The Inky Pink
Be Bopper

The inky pink be bopper
slid by me
in violet clothes
punctuated and dedicated
with
delicate prose.

She glided by
then stopped
in silent
repose.

I didn't think I would like
be boppers in violet clothes.

Must have been the prose
that put her fashions in vogue.

So when it comes to
inky pink be boppers,
one never knows...
I suppose.

The Lilies

The lilies
walked embarrassed
sideways
with
introverted smiles.

Legs caressed
in rococo socks
highlighted the vacuum
of their lips
otherwise
too
thick.

Onward clopping
came the lilies.
The stares they made
fearful, helpless
ending afraid-

Made me feel silly
but glad
don't wave.

The One of Day

Suddenly
came the one of day
the scrambling tooth pickers
on stilts
were scurrying casually
frantic still.

Happy
like a posse of wild giraffes
shooting arrows
at wagon trains
but no one shot arrows.

Faster and vaster
went the wooden sheep herd
looking more and more
like ants
than thinkers
hustling like armies
they marched on
across sidewalks
that reeked of similarity
and they disgraced them not.

Lovely Stranger

Hyper ek mon muniate
my cow bowah!
Ears ah lovely stranger
and pardon the danger
that effervesces
from your pineapple face
yerself.

Mr. Poppy and Me

The very mousy Mrs. Maybe
wasn't
what it was
and this is not a lonely night
to be willowing your ties away.

You're in a dream
and you seem like
Mr. Merry Gold.
Me
thinks
I'll paraphrase.
"Your marmalade
is on my tie."

Hello to Mrs. Poppy.
have ya
got
a word
for me?

I understand Sheila Winter
is in a song
and sings a pretty melody
a melodic line that
circles and rhymes
and sails and glides
like the most cylindrical waves
on
a sea of
sarsaparilla.

Jeepers!

Oh, Mr. Poppy, try to believe in
the man I am
a Merry Gold,
very
nice man.

Mr. Poppy my friend-
try not to pretend
and remember to mend your sleeve
with stardust
and you will perceive
and be true to beginning
the believing beguine, I mean.

Hooray for Mr. Poppy
Hooray for Mr. Me.
Conceived on this 26th day of March
somewhere
in
eternity.

Ode to
The Enchanted Sailing Man

Oh, shant entranted ode.
Trant I know not
the entertwinings of yer mind.
Schweep me with ye mittens, matie.
And a hoot, toot, tea too
to you
my flag.

I'm an ole sailor of some I am.
And a hoot, toot, tea too
my flag.

Hort tea snort tea snort tea.
Worn't ya used to the rugged way
me matie?

Can you add to me crew, me man?

Oh, hort tea; snort tea, snort tea.
I'm an ole sailor of some I am.

I'm 'n got me face on a flag.
Hort tea; snort tea snort.
Kablam.

The End

About the Author

Ron Bartalini was born and raised in California. He has written another book of poetry, *"I Like You Because You Make Me Happy."* He is also the author of, *"My Greatest Love, Missionary Stories from My Life"* and *"Hoppity Moose and the Red* Caboose." He currently resides in Utah.

www.ingramcontent.com/pod-product-compliance
Lightning Source LLC
LaVergne TN
LVHW051643080426
835511LV00016B/2470